Baseball's Best

Phil Kettle
illustrated by Craig Smith

Distributed in
the United States of America
by Pacific Learning
P.O. Box 2723
Huntington Beach, CA
92647-0723

Website:
www.pacificlearning.com

Published by Black Hills
(an imprint of Toocool Rules
Pty Ltd)
PO Box 2073
Fitzroy MDC VIC 3065
Australia
61+3+9419-9406

First published in the United States by Black Hills in 2004.
American editorial by Pacific Learning in 2004.
Text copyright © Phillip Kettle, 2002.
Illustration copyright © Toocool Rules Pty Limited, 2002.

 a black dog and Springhill book

Printed in China through Colorcraft Ltd, Hong Kong

ISBN 978 1 920924 13 3
PL-6208

10 9 8 7 6 5 4 3   09 08 07

Contents

Roberto

Marcy

Mr. Lopez

Tony

Gemma

Dan

Simon

Dog

Eddie

Toocool

Chapter 1

Wham!

Marcy was showing us what she would do to the ball at the game tomorrow.

"I'll splatter it like a lemon," she yelled.

She swung the bat. Wham! The lemon left the tree like a rocket. It shot straight up over the fence.

Mr. Lopez's head popped up. He was covered in splattered lemon.

"This is like a war zone," he said. "Get your bikes. We're going to the park. You kids need one more practice before tomorrow's big game."

Yes! We'd hoped he would say that.

At the park, Mr. Lopez
lined us up for catching
practice. As usual, I was in
great form. I caught every ball.
My hands were like a steel trap.
I knew Mr. Lopez would pick
me to be captain.

"We're in great shape," Mr.
Lopez said. "The Westside
Winners don't have a chance!"

I asked if I was going to be captain.

"You'd be a great captain, Toocool," said Mr. Lopez.

I couldn't stop smiling until he said, "I want Roberto to be captain this time. The rest of you have to help him."

Roberto! How could Mr. Lopez think Roberto would be a better captain than I would?

Chapter 2
The Team

I woke up early. It's always hard for me to sleep before a big game. It must be the pressure of being a star player.

Dog was waiting for me. His tail was wagging so fast, I couldn't see it.

When I got to Toocool
Park, the rest of my team
was already there. Simon had
his lucky mitt. He was our
catcher. Marcy was swinging her
bat. She was all fired up.
Roberto was showing Eddie and
Dan how to slide.

I rode through the gates and waited for the cheers.

"Hurry up, Toocool!" yelled Roberto. "We thought you overslept. We were terrified that Dog wouldn't make it to the game."

Marcy grabbed Dog.

"Dog, we want you to wear this," she said. She put a Legends T-shirt on Dog. We thought he looked cool, but he ripped it off right away.

Roberto said he wanted me to be pitcher.

Roberto was a bossy captain, but at least he knew who the star pitcher was.

Chapter 3
The Big Game

The birds stopped chirping. The crowd became quiet. Even Dog froze in his tracks.

The Westside Winners had arrived. The captain walked toward us. He had a lollipop sticking out of his mouth.

"Who's your captain?" he growled.

We quickly pushed Roberto toward him.

"He is!" we all yelled.

"You bat first—and no funny business this time," the Winners' captain snarled.

He was looking at Dog when he said that.

Roberto agreed we would
bat first. If I had been captain,
I wouldn't have let them boss
me around. Of course,
Roberto's not as tough as I am.

Mr. Lopez called us over.

"Let's show them how real
champs play," he said.

I stepped up to home plate.
I swung the bat around my
shoulders. I had to make sure I
was warmed up.

"Come on, tough guy,"
yelled the pitcher. "I'm going to
strike you out in a flash."

I gave him a Toocool stare.

He pitched the first ball. It came like a comet. I hit it hard. I started to run.

There was no need to run. The ball flew straight back into the pitcher's mitt.

I was out! I could not believe it!

The pitcher threw his mitt in the air. He must have felt very lucky.

I was sure no one had ever caught one of my fly balls before.

Chapter 4
Roberto Saves the Day

For a while, we looked good. Marcy hit a home run. Roberto got to third base. The rest of the team never left home plate. I knew that only my star pitching would save us.

(15)

The Winners' first batter stepped up to the plate.

I stood on the mound.

"Throw him a slow ball," whispered Roberto.

I decided to throw him a curveball. What did Roberto know about pitching?

I took aim and threw. It was a perfect curveball, but the batter got lucky. He slammed the ball. It went straight over the fence.

Dog took off after it, but he was too late.

It was a home run.

Roberto and Marcy started yelling at me. Mr. Lopez called me over.

I had to promise to do what Roberto said. After all, Roberto was captain.

The game was tied. The next batter came up to the plate. Roberto nodded at me. I knew what to do.

I pitched as hard as I could. There were flames coming from the ball. Somehow the batter hit it! It fired into the outfield.

Dog took off running. He scooped up the ball in his mouth. He ran toward home base. The batter was running at top speed. Dog was almost flying! He landed right in the middle of home plate.

The batter tried to slide, but it was too late. Dog stood over him. He dropped the ball on the batter's chest.

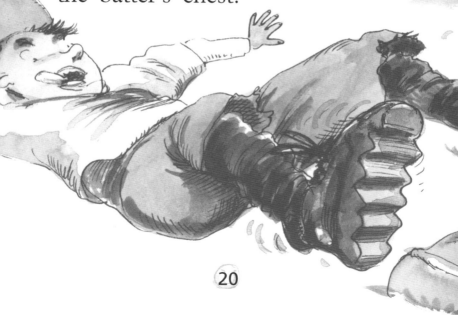

The Winners started booing.
The captain marched toward
me. He knew Dog belonged
to me.

"You can't have that dog on
your team!" he yelled.

He looked really mad. This was going to be ugly. I was a little worried. It had not been a good day.

Roberto stepped between me and the Winners' captain. Roberto said that Dog was an official team member. He said the Winners knew that Dog was always on our team.

The captain threw his hat down. He was going to quit. Then Roberto announced that the Winners could have a dog on their team, too.

The captain liked that idea.
He calmed down. He called for
the game to continue.

Roberto had saved the day.

I could not have done any
better myself.

Chapter 5
Tie Game

o one scored after that. Dog lost interest in the game. He fell asleep under a tree.

In the end, Mr. Lopez declared a tie.

The Winners said they would have a special team member at the next game.

We wondered what kind of dog they would have.

Simon said it would probably be a miniature poodle.

I had played really well, but it had not been our best game. Mr. Lopez said we all had played like champs. He's a good coach.

Roberto's a pretty good captain, too. I'd trust his help on any project I might ever try. The End!

Toocool's
Baseball Glossary

Catcher—The player who is behind the batter and catches the ball after it is thrown by the pitcher.

Home plate—This is where the batter starts and finishes. The batter steps up to the plate to hit the ball. If the batter makes it around all the bases, then tags home plate, a run is scored. Home plate is also called home base.

Mound—The small hill that the pitcher stands on to throw the ball.

Pitcher—The player who throws the ball to the batter.

Toocool's Map
The Baseball Field

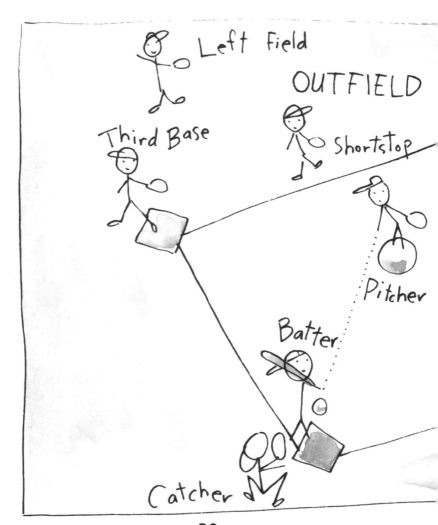

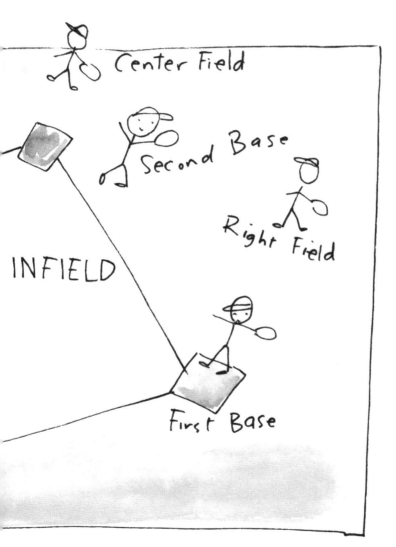

Center Field

Second Base

Right Field

INFIELD

First Base

31

Toocool's Quick Summary
Baseball

Baseball is a fantastic game. It is really popular. Some people even call it our national pastime. One of the great things about baseball is that there are lots of opportunities for kids to play the game.

Professional baseball is played by teams of nine players on a big field. The bases are placed around a diamond-shaped infield. Each base is on a corner of the diamond. The field outside of the bases is called the outfield.

One of the best ways to play baseball is with friends. When you play with friends, it doesn't matter how many people play. The field can be any size you want—as long as you have four bases to run around. You also need a bat and a ball. The rules are simple. Try to hit the ball, run around each base, and score a run for your team.

Remember, though, three strikes and you're out! If the ball is caught on the fly, you're out! If the ball gets to the base player before you get to that base, you're out! When you play baseball with your friends, the best rule is that anyone can play—even dogs.

The Legends

Q & A with **Toocool**
He Answers His Own Questions

🅑 **Do you have a favorite position to play?**

I can play anywhere because I'm good at all positions—both infield and outfield. I'm an excellent pitcher. I try to make my pitches unhittable, but sometimes the batters get lucky. I'm also a great catcher because my mitt is like a steel trap. Simon is our catcher only because I can't be everywhere at once.

What is a strike?

A strike is when the batter swings at the ball but misses. I'm an excellent pitcher, so I'm really good at pitching the ball in the strike zone. This means the pitch is a strike even if the batter doesn't swing at the ball.

Who is the best batter on the Legends baseball team?

I am the best batter. Marcy has hit the most home runs, but that doesn't mean anything. She's just lucky. When she hits the ball, the outfielders watch it soar over their heads. When I hit the ball, everyone makes a huge effort to catch it. They think it's a pretty big deal to get me out.

Have you ever hit a home run?

Yes, of course. There was one special one, though. The bases were loaded. It was my turn to bat. I had already swung once and missed, but I wasn't quite warmed up. I took a huge swing at the next ball, and WHAM! The ball flew past the infielders and way into left field.

Marcy, Roberto, and Eddie all made it to home base. Their cheers were so loud I didn't hear the umpire call "foul ball." We all celebrated when I tagged home plate. We still talk about what a great day that was.

Did it take you long to learn how to pitch?

No, I'm a natural.

Do you have any tips for your fans?

Yes. I would like to make a statement to all my fans.

Today, the Legends were honored to have me on their team. Without me, they would not have been as good. We were unlucky. The next time we play the Westside Whiners, we will definitely win.

We intend to keep training hard at TC Park—the home of the Legends. If you want to be like me—one of baseball's best—you have to practice, practice, practice.

Baseball Quiz
How Much Do You Know about Baseball?

Q1 What is a catcher?
A. A person who plays behind home plate. *B.* A person who catches the most balls at practice. *C.* A person who catches stray dogs.

Q2 How many bases are there on a baseball field?
A. One. *B.* Three. *C.* Four.

40

Q3 What does it mean if the bases are loaded?
A. The game is over and the bases have been loaded into Mr. Lopez's car. *B.* The bases are covered in dirt. *C.* There is one runner each on first, second, and third base.

Q4 Where is the strike zone?
A. In the outfield. *B.* Between the batter's armpits and knees.
C. Anyplace Marcy tries to hit with her bat.

Q5 What is a grounder?
A. When you hit the dirt, face first. *B.* When the ball hits the ground after you hit it. *C.* A small animal that lives in a burrow.

Q6 What does it mean if you have three strikes?
A. You have been hit by the ball three times. *B.* You're out! *C.* You have hit three home runs.

Q7 What is a full count?
A. Three balls and two strikes. *B.* Ten out of ten. *C.* Too much lemonade.

Q8 What is a foul ball?
A. A ball that smells bad. *B.* A dance for chickens. *C.* A ball that is hit outside the playing area.

Q9 How many people are on a baseball team?
A. Nine. *B.* As many as you can find. *C.* Six people and one dog.

Q10 Who is the best baseball player?

A. Toocool. **B.** Marcy. **C.** Dog.

ANSWERS

1 A.   **2** C.   **3** C.

4 B.   **5** B.   **6** B.

7 A.   **8** C.   **9** A.

10 A.

If you got ten questions right, you could be a team captain one day. If you got more than five right, you're still in the outfield. If you got fewer than five right, stick to jigsaw puzzles.

TOO COOL

Water Slide Winner

Toocool has built the best water slide in the world. Now he's set to be the fastest water slider in the world. It's a race against Marcy, Roberto, and the stopwatch.

Titles in the Toocool series

Slam Dunk Magician

Fishing Fanatic

BMX Champ

Surfing Pro

Tennis Ace

Skateboard Standout

Golfing Giant

Football Legend

Sonic Mountain Bike

Supreme Sailor

Gocart Genius

Invincible Iron Man

Soccer Superstar

Baseball's Best

Water Slide Winner

Beach Patrol

Rodeo Cowboy

Space Captain

Daredevil on Ice

Discus Dynamo